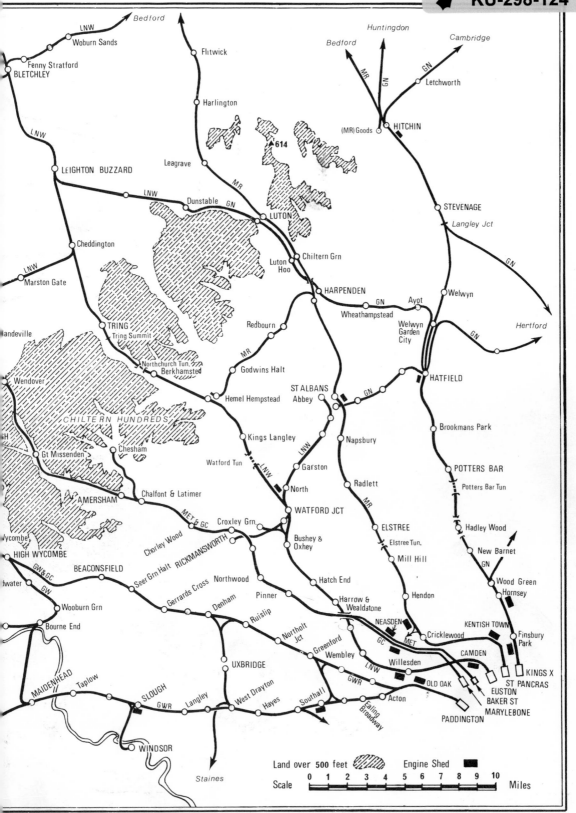

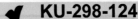

Railways
through the
CHILTERNS

COLES, C.R.L.

Railways through the Chilterns

This book is due for return on or before the last date shown above but it may be renewed unless required by other readers, by personal application, post, or telephone, quoting this date and the author and title.

Railways
through the
CHILTERNS

C.R.L.COLES

LONDON
IAN ALLAN LTD

Title page: The 6.10pm express from Paddington to Birkenhead passing Gerrards Cross in 1946 headed by 'King' class 4-6-0 No 6011 *King James I.*

First published 1980

ISBN 0 7110 1067 6

Published by Ian Allan Ltd, Shepperton, Surrey; and printed by Ian Allan Printing Ltd at their works at Coombelands in Runnymede, England

Introduction

The Chilterns, together with their ancient highways of which the best known — The Icknield Way — dates back to Roman times, are part of a band of chalk country which extends across southern and eastern England from Salisbury Plain to that part of the Norfolk coast lying a little to the east of the Wash. They embrace parts of five counties — Beds, Bucks, Herts, Middlesex (now Greater London) and Oxon; are more than 50 miles long and, at their broadest between the Staines and Aylesbury valleys, are about 30 miles wide. Within that area a somewhat narrower ridge of downland with a relatively steep escarpment on its western face extends from the Thames Valley at Streatley to Stokenchurch, Wendover, Ivinghoe and beyond to Dunstable and Hitchin east of which the contours are rather more isolated yet, in places, too steep for the plough. Thus the River Thames forms the natural boundary between the Chiltern Hills and the chalk downland west of Streatley. The eastern boundary is less easy to define. Here, the chalk band extends in places to between 10 and 20 miles from London — much of it being covered with glacial drift in varying depths with the exception of a small area a little to the west of Ruislip where the chalk is quite near to the surface. Thus there is justification for regarding the area west of a line drawn from Ruislip through Bushey to St Albans as being Chiltern country. Some geographers even include Hertford, principally because it, too, lies within the chalk strip and is on the direct approach to the downs near Dunstable. I am inclined to support that opinion; others might differ. In general, the downs rise to between 500 and 600ft above sea level though some of the higher points are over 800ft above ordnance datum — Coombe Hill, overlooking Wendover being the highest point (852ft). Some of the finest beechwoods in England are to be found on the lower slopes. These woodlands are rich in wild flora including the very rare Military Orchid. For obvious reasons the exact locations of this and other rare species of wild flowers remain a closely guarded secret. Apart from that isolated area near Ruislip, it is only on the downs and in the escarpment areas that the chalk is near to the surface. Here, too, many species of chalk flowers, some of which are quite rare, are to be found — especially in railway cuttings which offer much protection to wild life from the ravages of man.

But this is an album of railway photographs taken in and around the Chilterns. Yet I make no apology for discussing some of the topographical features of this part of England. A born countryman, on my many trips into this part of the country in search of interesting railway photographs, it has been an added pleasure between trains to enjoy to the full some of the beauties of nature which the Almighty has given to us all.

Turning now to the railways serving Chiltern country, all follow the valleys that intersect the hills in a south-easterly direction. Of these, the former LNWR and Midland still retain the status of main trunk routes between London and the north. The two arms of the former Great Central system which were jointly owned by the Metropolitan Railway on the one hand and the Great Western on the other likewise enjoyed main line status until long distance trains to and from Marylebone were withdrawn in the late 1950s. The Wycombe route however continued to be used by the Western Region of British Railways for its principal express services between London, Birmingham, Shrewsbury and the Cambrian Coast until late 1963 or perhaps even later. During this period the principal express between Paddington and Birmingham was the diesel operated 'Birmingham Pullman' and this provided the fastest service between these two cities during the period that the main line from Euston was being electrified. Today both the Wycombe line and the Metropolitan line via Rickmansworth have been relegated to short distance passenger trains to and from London (with the exception of one or two expresses to and from Birmingham, which are still routed via High Wycombe) and occasional long distance special excursions. Oil trains from the refineries at Thames Haven and the Isle of Grain also use this route on their journeys to and from the installations at Thame as do supplies of coal and gypsum to the cement works at Chinnor.

I have always held the view that, in their heyday as main lines, these two joint lines were more interesting than the LNW and Midland routes. Not only over a period of years was it possible to record a greater variety of locomotives, but the scenery is, to me, rather more attractive and less industrialised. This is especially the case on the Wycombe route where the several deep cuttings are spanned by high wide arched overbridges all built with blue-grey brick. These bridges are graceful to look at and harmonise with the surrounding countryside.

There remain three other routes which can justly claim to be associated with Chiltern country. Between Reading and Didcot the main line from Paddington to Bristol skirts the southern fringe of these hills as also does the main line from Kings Cross encroach upon the eastern shoulders in the vicinity of Stevenage and Hitchin whilst the former Great Eastern Railway gained access to the Chilterns via the Lea Valley.

Coming now to the period covered by this collection of photographs, the most interesting is by far the first 10 years following the Grouping in 1923. Although it was not until the early 1930s that I was in a position to start building up my collection of railway photographs, I have been able to record many changes between then and the outbreak of World War 2 in September 1939. Many of the older pre-Grouping locomotive classes were being withdrawn from service whilst others were performing less arduous duties. This was most noticeable on the main line from Euston to Crewe and beyond especially after the introduction of the 'Royal Scot' class in 1927. Even so the older 'Claughton' class engines still undertook a fair share of main line duties and for which a number were provided with larger boilers. But on the other main lines — more especially the former Midland and GC routes to and from London, the older pre-Grouping express passenger classes continued to perform regular main line duties well into the late 1930s before they, too, were largely superseded by locomotives of more modern design.

Except for one isolated occasion in 1944 when I was able to record the sight of an American-built austerity 2-8-0 on a mixed freight train, I now come to the postwar period and, with it, Nationalisation. Between 1945 and the beginning of 1948 when Britain's railways came under public ownership, the somewhat drab and austere appearance of locomotives and trains was gradually giving way to a new look. But with Nationalisation, this particular face-lift became short lived. Instead, we were to witness a range of experimental liveries which were widely publicised and which would eventually lead to some form of standardisation as far as the outward appearance of locomotives and rolling stock was concerned. In that same year yet another event of exceptional interest to all railway connoisseurs was to take place — the locomotive exchange trials. It has been said that these trials may have paved the way for the subsequent introduction of the British Railways standard classes — altogether 12 in number — of which the 'Britannia' 4-6-2s are the best remembered. It was No 70004 of this class named *William Shakespeare* that was exhibited at the Festival of Britain Exhibition on the South Bank of the River Thames in London during 1951.

Meanwhile the forerunner of main line diesel-electric locomotives, No 10000, was already running between Derby and St Pancras. I first photographed this locomotive in 1947 at Elstree when hauling an express from Manchester to St Pancras. Two more designs were soon to follow the two Derby-built locomotives — one from Eastleigh; the other from the English Electric Company Ltd. Both were tried out on express passenger services between Euston and the north. Clearly the transition from steam to electric and diesel traction was taking place. A few more years and, apart from nostalgic and other special duties, the sight of a steam hauled train would become no more than a memory. In the Chilterns, London Transport were quadrupling the Metropolitan line between Harrow and Watford South Junction whilst electrification northward from Rickmansworth to Amersham and Chesham was also in progress. Thus there was much to record with the camera during this period of railway modernisation.

In this pictorial collection of photographs, I have, after much thought and consideration, decided to include the approaches to the Chilterns mainly from the Metropolis — London's green belt in Middlesex and Herts merges into the eastern fringe of Chiltern country. Beyond the chalk escarpment, the line between Oxford and Bedford provided, at one time, direct contact with the four main routes through the Chilterns as well as with the Thames Valley line via Reading. It also provided an indirect link via Luton and Welwyn Garden City with the main line from Kings Cross. Within this perimeter (and including the Hertford loop line), a somewhat more flexible approach, which I considered desirable, has enabled me to present a wider picture of the area as a whole than would be the case had I to confine myself solely to the lines within Chiltern boundaries. Hence the inclusion of a few pictures taken on this cross-country route of which, today, only the section between Bletchley and Bedford remains open for passenger traffic.

Which brings me now to Metroland — the name given to that part of the country served by the outer arm of the former Metropolitan Railway of which the two rural extremities — to Brill and Verney Junction — were always looked upon as a part of the Chiltern scene. They still are despite the fact that, beyond Quainton Road station (now the headquarters of the Quainton Railway Society Ltd), both branches no longer exist. The story of the Metropolitan has been so admirably told elsewhere that I need do no more than make a passing reference to it here.

I have also included certain other branch lines which themselves are, in more ways than one, no less interesting. Some still survive; others alas no longer exist apart from stretches of track bed, the odd bridge here and there, and the remains of station buildings and signalboxes for which, in some cases, other uses have been found.

To assemble and arrange a series of photographs taken over a period of a little more than 30 years from the early 1930s until the almost complete eclipse of steam in the first half of the 1960s has been a most enjoyable task. I have also included a few pictures of somewhat older vintage where I have felt that these are of more than usual interest. The chief difficulty has been to decide what has had to be omitted from the material at my disposal. Except on the Midland division of the former LMSR, where a few photographs recalling the introduction of larger and more powerful locomotives from the time of the Grouping until the demise of steam have been arranged in chronological order, I have arranged the photographs in three separate groups such that, in sequence, each one constitutes an imaginary round tour — outward from London by one route and returning by another. As the pictures have been taken over a wide period of years, it has not been possible to arrange them in date order. Each of the three groups is prefaced by a synopsis of the routes and locations including, where applicable, items of historic interest. Accent has been on variety, not only as regards different locomotive classes (more than 80 are represented in this album) but unusual train workings, seasonal cross-country holiday services, weekend track repairs, bridge reconstruction and so forth. Even the one-time familiar short distance pick-up goods train, generally in charge of a veteran pre-Grouping locomotive, deserves a place in an album such as this. Railway landscape too, has not escaped attention. Here I refer to bridges, tunnel mouths, station architecture, track layout, signal gantries etc all of which contribute to the railway scene as a whole.

Most of the photographs are of my own taking. There are, however, a few stretches of railway in the Chilterns on which, for one reason or another, I never had the opportunity to photograph steam trains until it was too late! I am therefore greatly indebted to a number of other contributors who, between them, either directly or indirectly, have enabled me to fill some of these gaps and whose names appear beneath their respective photographs. Without this cooperation it would not have been possible to produce as complete a pictorial survey as here presented.

One feature which I would have liked to photograph concerned the 7.10pm express from Paddington to Wolverhampton. As late as June 1956, this train conveyed a slip portion which was detached at Princes Risborough from which it was worked forward to Banbury by an 0-6-0PT locomotive calling at all stations. Because of the time of evening, it would only have been possible to obtain a satisfactory negative during the summer and even then only when weather conditions were sufficiently favourable. Here I would like to express my thanks to the Editor of the *Bucks Advertiser and Aylesbury News* for his efforts in an endeavour to find a photograph of this operation but without success. This was the last of its kind on British Railways and, for that reason alone, is worthy of mention. Fortunately, this has been very successfully recorded on tape if not by the camera.

I also extend my thanks to following:

Mr J. P. Darling of Southall who has made a detailed study of the former GWR auto-trains at one time operating in the London area and who has given me some very interesting information concerning the alphabetical duty codes displayed by these units.

Mr D. Edwards of Ickenham for detail of environmental developments in and around Hemel Hempstead during the last decade particularly that part of the area served by the former Midland Railway branch from Harpenden.

The Librarian at Hillingdon Borough Library, Uxbridge, for facilities extended to me in search of material concerning the former branch between Denham and Uxbridge (High Street).

The London Transport Publicity Officer at Griffiths House, London NW1 for facilities accorded to me in enabling me to peruse through their extensive pictorial library.

Finally, all my other friends too numerous to mention individually who have helped me with advice and information and from which I have benefited considerably.

With the odd exception here and there, I have omitted main line diesel traction other than the two Pullman expresses serving Birmingham and Manchester both of which were short lived. On the other hand I have included pictures taken on the London Transport electrified lines which, I feel, are of more than usual interest. In the London area, steam lingered on until the middle 1960s — one of the last trains to be steam hauled being the 4.15pm semi-fast from Paddington to Banbury. It is with the picture of 'Castle' class 4-6-0 No 7029 *Clun Castle* at the head of this train between Beaconsfield and High Wycombe on 11 June 1965 that I bring this pictorial survey to a close.

Ruislip, Middx
January 1980

C. R. L. Coles

Select Bibliography

Baker, C.; *The Metropolitan Railway;* Oakwood Press, 1951.

Bonnett, Harold; 'Minerals to Chinnor', *The Railway Magazine;* August 1979.

Cockman, F. C.; *The Railways of Hertfordshire;* Hertfordshire Library Service in association with Hertfordshire Local History Council, 1978

Edwards, Dennis, and Pigram, Ron; *Metro Memories;* Midas Books, 1977.

Edwards, Dennis, and Pigram, Ron; *The Romance of Metroland;* Midas Books, 1979.

Hamilton Ellis, C.; *The Midland Railway;* Ian Allan Ltd, 1953.

Spencer Gilks, J.; 'The Hertford, Luton & Dunstable Railway', *Railway World;* January 1961.

Lindgard, Richard; *Princes Risborough-Thame-Oxford Railway;* Oxford Publishing Co, 1978.

Lousley, C. E.; *Wild Flowers of Chalk and Limestone;* Collins, 1950.

Massingham, H. J.; *English Downland;* B. T. Batsford Ltd, 1942/43.

Nock, O. S.; *Premier Line;* Ian Allan Ltd, 1973.

Nock, O. S.; *British Railways in Action;* Thomas Nelson & Sons Ltd, 1956.

Nock, O. S.; *60 years of Western Express Running;* Ian Allan Ltd, 1973.

Simpson, Bill; *The Banbury to Verney Junction Branch;* Oxford Publishing Co, 1978.

Dudley Stamp, L.; *Britain's Structure & Scenery;* Collins, 1946.

Woodward, G. S.; *The Hatfield, Luton & Dunstable Railway* (and on to Leighton Buzzard); The Oakwood Press, 1977.

Long Playing Records — 12 inch

Handford, Peter; *The Great Western;* Record No DA 39; Argo Record Co Ltd, 1966.

Symes-Schutzmann, R. A.; *The End of Steam;* Record No REB 30; BBC Radio Enterprises.

Ordnance Survey Maps — Scale One Inch to One Mile. Sheet 160; 1947 and later editions.

Bartholomew's Revised 'Half-Inch' Contoured Map — Sheet No 25, Herts & Bucks.

London to Oxford via the Thames Valley and returning to Marylebone via Princes Risborough

Starting from Paddington we take the West of England main line at Old Oak Junction West near which was, in the days of steam, London's largest locomotive depot and continued to Maidenhead for a trip on the branch to Bourne End and Marlow. The nine-mile stretch of the River Thames from here to Henley-on-Thames with the Chiltern Hills on the right can be made by boat. If we are lucky, we might, on our way upstream catch sight of a kingfisher — one of Britain's protected species of wild birds. We then continue via Goring to Didcot (headquarters of the Great Western Society Limited) and Oxford.

I have always held the view that, with the development of the motor industry at Morris Cowley and the admission by the Football League of Oxford United FC into Division IV some years ago, it would have been possible to popularise the direct cross-country link between Oxford and Princes Risborough as a viable concern. But this was not to be. Passenger traffic over this branch ceased at the beginning of 1963 and today, only the sections between Oxford and Morris Cowley and eastward of Thame remain intact, and for freight only. The rest of the branch has been lifted. Before closure, this line was sometimes used as an alternative route to and from Birmingham when weekend work on the main line via Ashendon Junction necessitated diversion of trains.

Ashendon Junction, nine miles north-west of Princes Risborough and where the former GC line to Rugby diverged to the right passing under the up GW line, no longer exists. The GC tracks have been removed as also has the up GW line including the girder bridge spanning the GC lines. Only the former down GW line has been retained — the section between Princes Risborough and Banbury being relegated to single line working.

At one time three branches deviated from the main line at Princes Risborough to Aylesbury, Oxford and Watlington. Only the Aylesbury branch enjoys a passenger service today. The Watlington branch, now only open for cement traffic to and from Chinnor, closely follows the western escarpment of the Chilterns. This branch was closed to passenger traffic in 1957.

From High Wycombe, which for a number of years has been associated with the furniture industry, the branch to Maidenhead diverged to the right of the main line and, crossing the A40 main road, continued on a downward gradient to Loudwater and Wooburn Green. The whole of this section as far as Bourne End no longer exists. It is also at High Wycombe that the well-known art printers, Harrison & Sons Ltd, produce Britain's postage stamps.

The branch to Uxbridge (High Street) left the GW&GC Joint Line at Denham East Junction. A curious feature of this line was the provision of locomotive watering facilities just beyond the junction stop signal. It must be assumed that, before closure in 1964, locomotives either proceeded light to this point to replenish their tanks or, alternatively, provision for this was allowed for in the working timetable on journeys between Uxbridge and Gerrards Cross. Today, little of this branch remains. A small bridge on the outskirts of Uxbridge which carried the line over a narrow lane and parts of the station buildings at Uxbridge are all that is left of what was once a country branch linking this town with the Chilterns.

A whole chapter could be written about Ruislip which, historically, is one of the most interesting places in this part of Greater London. At the time of the Norman Conquest it was known as 'The Manor of Rislepe' and, as such, is recorded in the Domesday Book. Today it is to West Ruislip station that new rolling stock for London Transport is brought by rail from the manufacturers; likewise it is from here that condemned Underground stock is despatched to the breakers yards.

Two miles further south we come to Northolt Junction (the station here is now named South Ruislip) where the up Marylebone line sweeps away to the left on a rising gradient of 1 in 180. The arrangement here is similar to that which once existed at Ashendon Junction except that the down line from Marylebone passes beneath the main line to and from Paddington which continues straight ahead.

Wembley Hill (since renamed Wembley Complex) is the last station before Marylebone. It is just beyond here that the GC line via Aylesbury, which at this point runs parallel to the Metropolitan line, is joined at Neasden South Junction. Until the main GC line was lifted some years ago, a most varied assortment of locomotives and rolling stock could be seen here on special excursions in conjunction with major sporting events at Wembley Stadium. This is reflected in my last picture in this group which shows a return excursion to Birmingham and Shrewsbury leaving Wembley Hill hauled by a former GW 'Hall' class 4-6-0.

Above: Paddington arrival. The red tail lamp has just been placed on the front buffer beam of 'Castle' class 4-6-0 No 5040 *Stokesay Castle* in readiness for backing out when the signal is given. To the left, passengers off the train await taxis. This picture was taken in April 1957. *C. R. L. Coles*

Below: Paddington departure. 'Saint' class 4-6-0 No 2980 *Coeur de Lion* displays the express passenger headcode in readiness to work a relief express to Birmingham. This photograph was taken in 1933 and, at that time, it was very unusual for an engine of this type to be seen on such duties — except at peak holiday periods. The Great Western 'Saints' were amongst the most handsome looking express passenger locomotives of their period. *C. R. L. Coles*

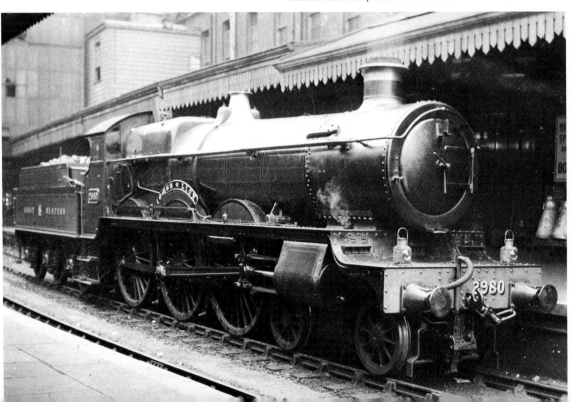

Left: 0-4-2T No 1421 at Bourne End (Bucks) with a train from Maidenhead to Marlow on 3 July 1962. This section of the former branch between Maidenhead and High Wycombe, together with the spur to Marlow, seen diverging to the right, remains in use today. *L. Nicholson*

Below left: Marlow station with 0-4-2T No 1448 and train on 21 June 1959. *C. R. L. Coles*

Right: The 6.55pm train from Maidenhead topping the summit between Cookham and Bourne End on 24 May 1962 headed by 61xx class 2-6-2T No 6164. The continuation of the branch between Bourne End and High Wycombe was closed completely in May 1970. *Gerald T. Robinson*

Below: Displaying the express passenger headcode, 'Castle' class 4-6-0 No 4096 *Highclere Castle* was photographed on 29 August 1962 leaving Wargrave with the 5.20pm from Paddington to Henley-on-Thames. *Gerald T. Robinson*

Left: The 8.30am express from Plymouth to Paddington was one of the trains selected to be hauled by 'foreign' locomotives during the exchange trials in 1948. LMR 'Duchess' class 4-6-2 No 46236 *City of Bradford* is here seen at the head of this express in Sonning Cutting in May 1948. *M. W. Earley*

Below left: 4-4-0 No 3440 *City of Truro* at the head of an RCTS special from Paddington to Swindon Works photographed in Sonning Cutting on 18 August 1957. *M. W. Earley*

Right: Southern Railway Class N15 4-6-0 No 784 *Sir Nerovens* at the head of a Bournemouth to Newcastle express passing over Goring Troughs in 1936. The line of trees on the left of this picture marks the southern fringe of the Chiltern Hills. *C. R. L. Coles*

Below: With a full head of steam, 'Castle' class 4-6-0 No 7017 *G. J. Churchward* awaits departure from Oxford with the 5.35pm express for Paddington in June 1958. At that time one through train each weekday used to run via the Thame branch to Princes Risborough and thence to Paddington. This train was generally hauled by either a 'Hall' or a 'Castle' class engine (see p25). *C. R. L. Coles*

Left: The 4.10pm (Sundays) express from Paddington to Birkenhead photographed near Morris Cowley on 11 September 1960. This train, headed by 'Hall' class 4-6-0 No 6934 *Beachamwell Hall*, which had called at High Wycombe, was diverted by the Thame branch because of engineering work on the direct route via Bicester. *M. Mensing*

Below: The 6.15pm train from Oxford to Princes Risborough photographed on 7 June 1958 taking water at Thame whilst waiting to cross another train bound for Oxford. *C. R. L. Coles*

Right: 'The Six Counties Ltd' special train organised by the Locomotive Club of Great Britain hauled by BR 2-10-0 No 92220 *Evening Star* at Princes Risborough on 3 April 1960. This train continued its tour via Thame to Oxford and beyond. *C. R. L. Coles*

Below right: An express freight train off the GC line passing Princes Risborough in April 1948 hauled by Gresley K3 class 2-6-0 No 61913. Former GW 2-6-2T No 6108 is engaged on shunting duties on the down platform line. *H. K. Harman*

Above: The 12.15pm express from Marylebone to Manchester hauled by Class A3 4-6-2 No 60111 *Enterprise* passing under the up GW line at Ashendon Junction on 26 July 1954. *Stanley Creer*

Below: The 1.10pm express from Paddington to Chester, headed by 4-6-0 No 5960 *Saint Edmund Hall* at Ashendon Junction on 27 August 1955. *Stanley Creer*

Princes Risborough-Watlington Branch

Above: Wainhill Crossing Halt looking towards Watlington. This section from Princes Risborough remains intact and is used for the conveyance of coal and gypsum to the cement works at Chinnor. *C. R. L. Coles*

Below: 0-6-0PT No 4650 at Watlington with a train from Princes Risborough on a sunny day in 1957. *M. J. Esau*

Saunderton Summit. The down and up lines here are on different inclinations — that of the former being the steeper (1 in 100-88-161) on the descent to Princes Risborough. The up line is an unbroken rise of 1 in 167 over a distance of nearly two miles between these two points. In these three photographs *(left)* former 'Star' class 4-6-0 No 4000 *North Star* (rebuilt as a 'Castle' class engine) is at the head of a relief portion of the 6.10pm express from Paddington which I photographed in May 1956; *(top)* 2-6-2T No 84008 with its one coach train was photographed at the same spot in July 1961; *(above)* on the up line an inter-city express from Birmingham to Paddington is headed by 4-6-0 No 5008 *Raglan Castle* in May 1956. *All C. R. L. Coles*

Above: 0-6-0PT No 6403 pushing the 9.45am (Sundays) train from High Wycombe to Aylesbury up the 1 in 164 gradient near Saunderton on 11 February 1962. *M. Pope*

Below: An unidentified 94xx 0-6-0PT passing Saunderton station with a down goods train in July 1961. *C. R. L. Coles*

Above right: LMR 'Duchess' class 4-6-2 No 46245 *City of London* photographed between West Wycombe and Saunderton on 1 September 1964 with an Ian Allan special from Paddington to Crewe works. *Gerald T. Robinson*

Right: The 11.10am express from Paddington to Wolverhampton approaching West Wycombe headed by 4-6-0 No 7013 *Bristol Castle* in 1950. *C. R. L. Coles*

Approaching High Wycombe

Although the natural valley which the railway follows runs in a south-easterly direction, High Wycombe is almost surrounded by hills — especially to the north of the town where the contours are generally very steep. This has necessitated the construction of a large retaining wall immediately west of the station and on the up side of the permanent way. These two photographs show how a change of view point, different lighting and camera equipment can produce different impressions of the same scene.

Above: The former GC 'Director' class 4-4-0 No 62666 *Zeebrugge* hauling a 'Northern Rubber Special' was photographed in weak sunshine on 6 June 1953. *C. R. L. Coles*

Below: The A4 Preservation Society special train from Manchester to Paddington was photographed in diffused daylight on 23 October 1965. The train is headed by A4 4-6-2 No 60007 *Sir Nigel Gresley*. *Brian Stephenson*

Left: 2-6-2T No 6167 with an up goods train near the site of West Wycombe station on 26 September 1964. In the left background stands West Wycombe church from which extensive views of the surrounding country may be had. The hill on which the church stands together with the charming village of West Wycombe (at the foot of the hill to the left of the church) are the property of the National Trust. *Brian Stephenson*

Left: As the driver sees it. A view from the front seat of a four coach diesel unit standing in the up platform at High Wycombe. These semaphore arms are of a significantly different pattern from that normally to be found in the vicinity. *C. R. L. Coles*

Below: Excursion train from Birmingham (Snow Hill) to Taplow headed by 4-6-0 No 7808 *Cookham Manor* photographed between High Wycombe and Beaconsfield on 17 September 1966. *Tim Stephens*

Right: 4-6-0 No 4938 *Liddington Hall* on Oxford to Paddington train via Thame approaching White House Farm Tunnel (between High Wycombe and Beaconsfield) in 1946. Note the set of 'Collett' articulated coaches. *C. R. L. Coles*

Below right: The 4.10pm express from Paddington to Birmingham and Wolverhampton headed by 'Star' class 4-6-0 No 4060 *Princess Eugenie* leaving White House Farm Tunnel in 1946. *C. R. L. Coles*

Above: Up Birkenhead to Paddington express near Seer Green hauled by 4-6-0 No 6008 *King James II*. Photographed in September 1938. *C. R. L. Coles*

Below: Robinson mixed traffic 4-6-0 No 5469 passing Seer Green with an excursion train off the GC line in September 1938. Train is composed of LNE green and white tourist stock. *C. R. L. Coles*

Right: Former GW 2-8-0 No 4701 passing Seer Green with an up goods train on 5 July 1952. *A. R. Carpenter*

Above left: Austerity 2-8-0 No 90174 approaching Beaconsfield with an up freight train on 28 September 1957. *K. L. Cook*

Left: 4-6-0 No 6976 *Graithwaite Hall* makes steady progress up the 1 in 264 between Gerrards Cross and Seer Green with the 4.10pm (Sundays) express from Paddington to Birmingham and beyond on 10 July 1955. *C. R. L. Coles*

Above: Former GC Robinson 4-6-0 No 5004 *Glenalmond* leaving Gerrards Cross with a down stopping train to High Wycombe and beyond in 1947. These engines were a small wheeled version of the well known 'Sir Sam Fay' class. *C. R. L. Coles*

Right: In immaculate external condition, ex-GC (Parker) 2-4-2T No 5727 pauses on the up through line at Gerrards Cross in 1936. I never saw this engine again and was unable to discover what duties it undertook or even where it was stationed. *C. R. L. Coles*

Above left: Paddington to High Wycombe train approaching Gerrards Cross hauled by 2-6-2T No 6126 in 1948. *C. R. L. Coles*

Left: Summer Saturday holiday traffic. Through train from Ramsgate to Nottingham approaching Gerrards Cross in September 1951 hauled by B1 class 4-6-0 No 61185. *C. R. L. Coles*

Above: High Wycombe to Marylebone stopping train leaving Gerrards Cross hauled by ex-GC A5 class 4-6-2T No 9810 in 1947. *C. R. L. Coles*

Right: Up goods train hauled by an unidentified 'Dukedog' 4-4-0 near Gerrards Cross in 1947. *C. R. L. Coles*

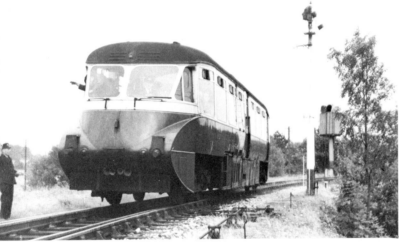

Above: An early photograph of Gerrards Cross station showing steam railcars Nos 8 and 31. It is believed that the year of this picture is not later than 1915. Of particular interest is the letter E on car No 8. In the London area these alphabetical codes denoted duty rosters from the time that a unit left its home depot until completing its scheduled duties. This system of code lettering lasted until after Nationalisation — possibly until the end of the steam era (see also p41). *Real Photographs Ltd*

Left: The branch to Uxbridge (High Street) diverged from the main line at Denham East Junction — the actual junction facing north. An unusual feature of this branch was the provision of watering facilities just beyond the stop signal instead of at the terminal points. This photograph was taken in September 1954 when the London Railway Society organised a rail tour of the branch by a former GWR diesel railcar. *C. R. L. Coles*

Bottom left: 2-6-2T No 5564 photographed in January 1964 when on shunting duty in the Uxbridge (High Street) coal depot. It is believed that this was the last occasion when a regular train travelled over this branch which officially closed in July 1964. *T. Wright*

Above right: Up excursion train from Leicester to Marylebone passing Denham in 1938 hauled by Class B17 4-6-0 No 2854 *Sunderland.* Speeds in excess of 90mph have been recorded here on a number of occasions. *C. R. L. Coles*

Right: The 4.10pm express from Paddington to Birmingham and Wolverhampton headed by 4-6-0 No 6001 *King Edward VII* passing the site of what was once South Harefield Halt. Photographed on 17 April 1955. *C. R. L. Coles*

Left: A cold northerly air stream was blowing down the cutting at South Harefield when I photographed the down 'Cambrian Coast Express' on 27 October 1956. The train is headed by 4-6-0 No 5087 *Tintern Abbey*, one of a batch of 'Castle' class locomotives which were rebuilt from earlier 'Star' class engines. *C. R. L. Coles*

Above: Former GC mixed traffic 4-6-0 No 5458 heading an up goods train near South Harefield in March 1938. *C. R. L. Coles*

Below: The 9.10am express from Paddington to Birmingham and Wolverhampton near South Harefield headed by 4-6-0 No 6014 *King Henry VII* as modified with bullet nose smokebox. Photograph taken in 1938. *C. R. L. Coles*

Above left: Down pick-up goods train approaching South Harefield in 1936 hauled by 'Dean' 0-6-0 No 2422.   *C. R. L. Coles*

Left: The 10am express from Marylebone to Manchester (London Road) approaching South Harefield in 1936 hauled by former GC 4-cylinder 4-6-0 No 6166 *Earl Haig*. In postwar years, this train was re-routed via Aylesbury.   *C. R. L. Coles*

Top: The down 'Birmingham Pullman' near West Ruislip in the early 1960s.   *C. R. L. Coles*

Above: The down 'Master Cutler' on Ruislip troughs headed by Standard Class 5 4-6-0 No 73156 on 8 June 1957.   *C. R. L. Coles*

Left: Track maintenance. Re-packing ballast on the down line under the water troughs at West Ruislip in 1952. *C. R. L. Coles*

Below: Return excursion from Wembley Hill to Leicester passing West Ruislip on 25 May 1963 headed by LMR 'Jubilee' class 4-6-0 No 45598 *Basutoland*. This particular class did not normally work over this line except on occasions such as this. *C. R. L. Coles*

Right: Weekend track repairs necessitating single line working. Class B1 4-6-0 No 61164 with a theatre special restarting 'wrong road' from West Ruislip due to occupation of the down line. Photographed on 13 February 1955. *C. R. L. Coles*

Below right: New stock for London Transport Piccadilly Line being delivered to the reception depot at West Ruislip by 2-6-2T No 6132. Photograph taken in September 1963. *C. R. L. Coles*

Left: Sometimes the unexpected happens! When running through the trap points on the up side of the approach to West Ruislip station, 0-6-0PT No 3799 became derailed. Inevitably there was some delay to up trains as the breakdown crane, when positioned, was blocking both the platform line and the up main line. Photograph taken on 9 February 1952. *C. R. L. Coles*

Above: Sandwiched between a pair of saloon type trailer coaches equipped for push and pull working, 0-6-0PT No 5401 was photographed at Ruislip & Ickenham in the mid-1930s. This station is now renamed West Ruislip. The letter F positioned in front of the chimney is believed to denote a duty code (see p32). *C. R. L. Coles*

Below: This is my only picture of an outside-framed 'Armstrong' 0-6-0 on one of its last duties. It is here seen at Ruislip & Ickenham in the early 1930s with an up pick-up goods train. *C. R. L. Coles*

Left: Down goods train restarting from West Ruislip after being held by signals. The locomotive is 'Star' class 4-6-0 No 4049 *Princess Maud*. The photograph was taken in 1949. *C. R. L. Coles*

When the bridge carrying the Paddington to Birmingham line over the London Transport Metropolitan line at West Ruislip necessitated complete renewal in May 1961, the work was undertaken such that traffic could be switched to the platform loops whilst the through lines were occupied — and vice versa. In the upper photograph both the up and down through lines are occupied. In the lower photograph an up express from Birmingham to Paddington headed by 4-6-0 No 5019 *Treago Castle* passes slowly by on the up platform loop. *Both C. R. L. Coles*

Left: The down 'Master Cutler' passing Ruislip Gardens in 1949 hauled by A3 class 4-6-2 No 60052 *Prince Palatine*. The locomotive is finished in the then new livery and is displaying the express passenger headcode by means of white discs instead of the customary lamps. *C. R. L. Coles*

Below left: Split distants near Ruislip Gardens. This signal gantry is of more than usual interest in that when photographed in 1950, provision was made for up trains to be switched from the up main to the up relief line beyond which, at Northolt Junction the Marylebone line diverges to the left whilst that for Paddington continues straight ahead. Track alterations since the photograph was taken have led to the removal of some of these semaphores and only the centre set now remains in use. *C. R. L. Coles*

Below: Up freight train hauled by an unidentified ex-GW 2-8-0 of the 28xx series passing a pw repair train near Ruislip Gardens in 1949. *C. R. L. Coles*

Bottom: The 6.10pm express from Paddington to Birkenhead passing South Ruislip in July 1956 headed by 4-6-0 No 6011 *King James I*. This photograph was awarded a certificate of merit in the 24th Kodak International Salon of Photography which was held in Rochester, NY in 1959. *C. R. L. Coles*

Above: The 12.15pm express from Marylebone to Manchester, hauled by A3 class 4-6-2 No 60059 *Tracery* passing under the main line from Paddington to Birmingham near South Ruislip on 19 April 1952. *C. R. L. Coles*

Left: Bridge renewal at South Ruislip in 1946. This photograph shows work in progress on the bridge carrying the main line from Paddington over the down line from Marylebone which joins the former at Northolt Junction, about 600yd further down. *C. R. L. Coles*

Right: Two photographs of the Ian Allan 'Pennine Pullman' approaching South Ruislip on 12 May 1956 hauled by A4 class 4-6-2 No 60014 *Silver Link*. *Both C. R. L. Coles*

Left: Up excursion from Bishop Auckland to Marylebone diverging from the joint line at Northolt Junction up a gradient of 1 in 180 towards Northolt Park on 10 April 1954. The locomotive is V2 class 2-6-2 No 60896. *C. R. L. Coles*

Above: Boat trains from Marylebone to Immingham Docks in conjunction with Norway cruises. These special trains ran on Fridays during the summer months and usually departed from London shortly before midday. They were routed via High Wycombe and were invariably hauled by a variety of ex-Great Central type locomotives. Sometimes the trains were double headed. In these two photographs both of which were taken at Northolt Park on successive Fridays during the summer of 1938, an 'Immingham' class 4-6-0 No 6095 is seen coasting down the gradient towards Northolt Junction with the regulator closed — hence the smoke drifting back over the train. The other photograph shows 4-6-0 No 5423 *Sir Sam Fay* at the head of the train. *Both C. R. L. Coles*

Above: Shortly after Nationalisation in 1948, ex-GWR 2-6-2T locomotives worked some suburban passenger trains between Marylebone, High Wycombe and Aylesbury. This arrangement did not last for very long. This photograph shows 2-6-2T No 6166 passing Sudbury Hill with a down train in 1949. *C. R. L. Coles*

Below: When major sporting events took place at Wembley Stadium, some of the return excursions in conjunction with these events commenced the return journey within two or three hours of the ending of such events. This photograph, taken on 26 April 1958, shows the 6.53pm to Shrewsbury headed by 4-6-0 No 6964 *Thornbridge Hall* leaving Wembley Hill — by which this station was, at that time, known. *C. R. L. Coles*

Through Metroland to Verney Junction; then Bletchley and returning to London via Tring

This part of Chiltern country is full of historical interest, railway and non-railway, some of which is worthy of mention in this preface to the second group of pictures.

From Baker Street we call first at Finchley Road which today is the inter-change point with the London Transport Jubilee Line — the outer end of which is the branch from Wembley Park to Stanmore. This was opened by the Metropolitan Railway in 1932. Prior to this there existed at Finchley Road station a physical connection with the LMSR (Midland Division) which also served a milk depot. In the late 1920s this link was regularly used for the transfer of milk vans to and from stations beyond Aylesbury. These vans were generally attached to certain passenger trains and I only wish that I could include a photograph showing them in transit. London Transport do not appear to have any such photographs in their archives and my only record of this (not suitable for reproduction) is on 16mm movie film. This depicts a rake of four or five such vans at the rear of an up train from Aylesbury.

As we continue through Neasden and Wembley Park towards Harrow, we see to our left the Parish Church of St Mary, surmounting Harrow Hill, which is a prominent landmark for many miles around. It is close to Harrow School where, at one time, Sir Winston Churchill was a scholar. Of the four branch lines still operational in outer Metroland, that from Harrow to Uxbridge is of more than usual interest. Though not the oldest (that distinction goes to the Chesham branch), it was opened in 1904 with one principal station at Ruislip, then a country village. Ruislip station has not been altered in outward appearance since it was first built. It is now scheduled for preservation as an example of Metropolitan station architecture. Steam hauled coal trains were to be regularly seen on this branch until regional distribution centres were set up by the National Coal Board and from which coal merchants now draw their supplies. Most of the space formerly taken up by coal wharfs at various stations on the branch have since been converted into car parks for commuter travellers.

In steam days, Rickmansworth was the change-over point between steam and electric traction — and vice-versa. Four minutes were normally allowed for this to take place. The station is on a sharp curve and on a rising gradient facing down trains. Violent slipping was, therefore, by no means uncommon especially in wet weather when the rails were somewhat greasy.

Chalfont & Latimer station is the junction for the Chesham branch which was opened in 1899. This runs parallel to the Aylesbury line for about a mile before diverging to the right. It is single throughout and, until September 1960, was steam operated. Close by is the village of Chalfont St Giles which is associated with John Milton who lived in a cottage in the village during the period of the Great Plague in London. It was here that the poet wrote part of *Paradise Regained*. We are now approaching what is sometimes referred to as the 'William Penn' country, so called because of its association with the most prominent Quaker in England. He lies buried in the grounds of Jordans Meeting House — a few miles away to our left.

Just before Wendover we reach the second of two summits, at Dutchlands — the first being at Amersham. To the left is Coombe Hill on the slopes of which lies Chequers Court, the official country residence of the Prime Minister. Wendover station is associated with an event which became one of the best kept secrets during World War 2. Early in the afternoon of Sunday, 3 August 1941, a special train left Marylebone conveying both dining and sleeping cars in its formation. The train stopped at Wendover where, on the platform, Sir Winston Churchill with his three chiefs of staff were waiting to join the train. Their destination was Thurso where the party boarded HMS *Prince of Wales* for their journey across the Atlantic to meet President Roosevelt at Placentia Bay, Newfoundland. In his book *British Railways in Action*, O. S. Nock has described this train as the Atlantic Charter Special.

So, on to Aylesbury, Quainton Road, Brill and Verney Junction to Bletchley. Continuing to Tring we pause first at Leighton Buzzard to cover the branch to Dunstable, then again at Cheddington for the former LMS branch to Aylesbury. Clankity, clankity, clankity, clank — that one time familiar staccato rhythm as the wheels passed over the short rail joints, characteristic of many country branch lines, was recorded by the BBC between Leighton Buzzard and Dunstable in 1951. Although neither of these branches exist today, this once familiar sound has been preserved for posterity.

It is just north of Tring that the chalk escarpment is reached and where the railway lies in a deep cutting — one of several nature reserves in this area. From Tring to Watford tunnel we are now in close company with the Grand Union Canal on our right. Today this inland waterway is mainly used for pleasure purposes though, at one time, not so very many years ago, a considerable amount of coal could still be seen on its way to London by barge. Watford Junction — change here for the St Albans (Abbey) branch. Change here also for the dc electrified suburban line to Euston and Broad Street via Watford (High Street) which, at one time, was also the junction for the Rickmansworth (Church Street) and Croxley Green branches. The former was closed to passenger traffic in March 1952 and to goods in January 1967 — apart from a section of line serving Dickinson's Paper Mill which is still open. On the Croxley Green branch, a passenger service now operates during Monday to Friday peak hours only. This same junction also gives access to the carriage sheds serving this suburban line. Then, over Bushey troughs for a final top-up and so to Harrow and Euston to witness the arrival of the up 'Caledonian' from Glasgow after its inaugural run in May 1957.

Top: Neasden (London Transport) Depot looking north. On the far left is the former GC line to Aylesbury and beyond. This joins the London Transport lines (left) at Harrow-on-the-Hill. On the right is the entrance to the car sheds and repair shops. Photograph taken in 1957. *C. R. L. Coles*

Above: Neasden (LT) power station in 1957 with 0-6-0ST No L53. Before the Metropolitan Railway became a part of the London Passenger Transport Board in 1933, this engine and another of the same type (in Metropolitan days they carried the numbers 101 and 102) were sometimes to be seen in Harrow goods yard. At that time there was an agreement between the then Metropolitan and the Great Central

companies for this and other duties to be shared in alternate five year periods. *C. R. L. Coles*

Right: Metropolitan Railway 4-4-0T No 23 as restored to its original condition on view at Neasden during the Metropolitan Centenary celebrations in May 1963. For many years, this and another of the same type, No 45, shared the working of the Brill branch. No 23 was built by Beyer Peacock & Co Ltd in 1864 who also built several similar type locomotives for the New South Wales Railway in Australia. Some of these veterans remained active until comparatively recently and one or two have since been preserved in working order. *C. R. L. Coles*

Above: Metropolitan H class 4-4-4T No 103 approaching Harrow-on-the-Hill in 1933. At that time this train ran non-stop between Great Missenden and Harrow, where the 4-4-4T was exchanged for one of the Metropolitan-Vickers 1,200hp electric locomotives for the continuation to Baker Street. This was the only steam hauled train on the Metropolitan system and worked by that company to carry the express passenger headcode on the buffer beam. *C. R. L. Coles*

Left: Former GC 'Director' class 4-4-0 No 5504 *Jutland* at Harrow-on-the-Hill on a stopping train from Leicester. At that time (1932/33) these engines were painted in the standard apple green livery adopted by the LNER for express passenger types. Later, as they went through the shops for overhaul, the 'Directors' re-emerged in black livery. *C. R. L. Coles*

Above right: Down Manchester express passing Harrow-on-the-Hill in 1948 hauled by 4-6-0 No E1298. This locomotive is painted in the former LNER apple green livery but inscribed BRITISH RAILWAYS on the tender sides. It also displays the prefix E to denote Eastern Region. Of the two GC routes from Marylebone, that via Aylesbury, though shorter in terms of mileage than the Wycombe route, was regarded as the more severe as regards gradients. *C. R. L. Coles*

Right: Metropolitan F class 0-6-2T No 91 with a rake of empty coal wagons off the Uxbridge branch photographed near the top of the flyunder at Harrow-on-the-Hill in 1933. The Aylesbury line is on the left. *C. R. L. Coles*

Above left: Materials train (pw department) photographed on 6 September 1952 between Ruislip Manor and Eastcote en route for Neasden from which it would subsequently be despatched to the tip sidings at Croxley. Except on the regular weekday working to Croxley, these trains were generally to be seen (and heard) at nightime or on Sundays wherever reballasting or other track maintenance work happened to be taking place. The locomotive is former F class 0-6-2T No L52 — London Transport numbering. On this occasion the train was returning from the Uxbridge end of the branch where work had been in progress earlier that day. *C. R. L. Coles*

Left: Metropolitan and Piccadilly line trains passing each other at Ruislip (Met) station. The station buildings and the footbridge are a fine example of Metropolitan station architecture and have been listed for

preservation. Photographed in September 1963. *C. R. L. Coles*

Top: Piccadilly line train photographed just after passing beneath the main line from Paddington to Birmingham. This photograph was taken in 1961 — the same year as was the bridge carrying the British Rail line reconstructed — p43. *C. R. L. Coles*

Above: From the bridge shown in the top picture I obtained this photograph of ex-GC 0-6-2T No 69315 with the daily coal train to stations on the Uxbridge branch where the local coal merchants had their wharfs. This is a 1949 picture since when the National Coal Board established regional distribution depots from which coal merchants now draw their supplies. At one time this duty was undertaken by the Metropolitan Railway — see p55. *C. R. L. Coles*

Left: The quadrupling of the Metropolitan line between Harrow and Watford South Junction necessitated the replacement of the old bridge carrying the railway over the A404 road at Northwood and which had always been a bottleneck. This photograph, taken in August 1960, shows the new railway bridge under construction. Opportunity was also taken at the same time to widen the carriageway and so eliminate the bottleneck. *C. R. L. Coles*

Top: During the locomotive exchange trials in 1948, the 10am express from Marylebone to Manchester was one of the selected trains which were hauled by 'foreign' locomotives. In this photograph, Southern

Region 'West Country' 4-6-2 No 34006 *Bude* with the former LNER dynomometer car next behind the LMR type tender (specially attached to the engine to permit taking water from track troughs), is shown passing Northwood. *C. R. L. Coles*

Above: Another Southern locomotive at the same place but some seven years later. Drummond T9 class 4-4-0 No 30719 was photographed on 15 May 1955 when heading a rambler's special from Waterloo to Great Missenden (named the 'William Penn Special'). This is believed to be the one and only occasion that an engine of this class ever travelled over the line. *C. R. L. Coles*

Left: Rickmansworth station is at the foot of the 1 in 105 climb to Amersham. It was here that before the line was electrified northwards to Amersham and Chesham, the change-over from steam to electric, and vice versa took place. Four minutes was the normal time for this to be accomplished. In this photograph, Metropolitan G class 0-6-4T No 94 *Lord Aberconway* had just started to draw ahead after being uncoupled from an up train from Aylesbury. This photograph was taken in 1937. *C. R. L. Coles*

Below: Metropolitan-Vickers 1,200hp electric locomotive leaving Rickmansworth on train for Liverpool Street in February 1952. The locomotive, No 14, carries the name *Benjamin Disraeli.* *C. R. L. Coles*

Right: Electric locomotive No 3 *Sir Ralph Verney* and No 4 *Lord Byron* in the sidings at Rickmansworth awaiting their next duty. Photographed on 2 September 1961. *C. R. L. Coles*

Below right: Up coal train entering the loop at Rickmansworth headed by Thompson B1 class 4-6-0 No 61317 in February 1952. *C. R. L. Coles*

Above: Although during the winter months London Transport takes steps to minimise the effects of adverse weather conditions, unexpected falls of snow can sometimes create havoc to scheduled train services — this being due to the formation of ice on the conductor rails as well as to frozen points. An electric train composed of A60 stock is here seen leaving Rickmansworth for Baker Street on a bright, cold, crisp winter's morning following a period of snow. *London Transport*

Left: The London Transport tip site at Croxley to which spoil and used ballast is taken at regular intervals. Photograph taken in April 1969 (see p56). *R. J. Greenaway*

Above right: In the heart of Metroland. A Metropolitan Railway H class 4-4-4T with a six-coach train of 'Dreadnought' stock is here seen near Chorley Wood storming up the 1 in 105 from Rickmansworth. This photograph is believed to have been taken in the late 1920s. *London Transport*

Right: On the Chesham branch. This photograph which was taken in 1950 shows ex-GCR 4-4-2T No 67418 and three coach train of London Transport Ashbury stock, fitted for push and pull working, approaching Chalfont & Latimer as it emerges from Quill Farm Wood. *C. R. L. Coles*

Above left: The 'John Milton Special' — organised for the benefit of ramblers, is here seen at Chesham on 3 June 1956. Metropolitan E class 0-4-4T No L48 had just run round the train in readiness for the return journey to Baker Street later in the day.   *C. R. L. Coles*

Left: Former GC 4-4-2 No 6085 with a train of milk empties is here seen between Chalfont & Latimer and Amersham in 1934. These

locomotives were nicknamed 'Jersey Lilies'.   *C. R. L. Coles*

Above: Down and up trains at Amersham. The former is being hauled by Stanier 2-6-4T No 42088; the up train by No 42256 of the same class. Both trains were composed of Metropolitan stock operating between Baker Street and Aylesbury and both were photographed on the same day — 11 September 1960.   *Both: C. R. L. Coles*

Above: In 1937 the Metropolitan Railway 4-4-4T locomotives were sold to the LNER by the London Passenger Transport Board. This photograph, taken in 1938 shows one of them renumbered 6415 near Little Missenden with a down train to Aylesbury composed of former Metropolitan stock. *C. R. L. Coles*

Below: Thompson Class L1 2-6-4T No 67747 near Great Missenden on an up train from Aylesbury to Marylebone in September 1951. *C. R. L. Coles*

Right: Former Metropolitan K class 2-6-4T No 115 near Dutchlands summit with an up goods train in 1938. This was one of six engines constructed for the Metropolitan Railway by Armstrong Whitworth & Co using parts which had been made at Woolwich Arsenal after World War 1. The locomotives were designed by George Hally. They possessed a distinctly 'Southern' appearance. *C. R. L. Coles*

Above left: Former GCR 2-6-4T No 69061 shunting wagons across the down line from Baker Street at Aylesbury in 1950. The line to Princes Risborough can be seen on the extreme right of the picture. *C. R. L. Coles*

Left: The up 'South Yorkshireman' hauled by B1 class 4-6-0 No 61156 approaching Aylesbury in 1950. *C. R. L. Coles*

Above: Aylesbury station looking towards London. This photograph was taken prior to 18 June 1962 when the subshed on the right was closed. In the adjacent platform is the 6.20pm train for Maidenhead, whilst on shed are 2-6-4T No 42090 and 2-6-2T No 84029 which was employed on the Princes Risborough to Chinnor freight duties. *Bryan S. Jennings*

Right: Cast iron notice plate outside Aylesbury station — photographed 5 May 1968. *Hugh B. Oliver*

GREAT WESTERN AND
GREAT CENTRAL RAILWAYS
JOINT COMMITTEE

METROPOLITAN AND GREAT
CENTRAL JOINT COMMITTEE

NOTICE IS HEREBY GIVEN
IN PURSUANCE OF THE PROVISIONS OF
SECTION 65 OF THE GREAT WESTERN RAILWAY
(ADDITIONAL POWERS) ACT 1924 AND
SECTION 70 OF THE LONDON AND NORTH EASTERN
RAILWAY ACT 1924 THAT
THIS IS A
PRIVATE ROAD

Above: Quainton Road station looking south towards Aylesbury and photographed in 1935. The former down line through the station has since been taken up as also has the siding beyond the station. A mixed train for Brill headed by a Beyer Peacock 4-4-0T locomotive, believed to be No 41, is to the right of the down platform the outer face of which served this branch. *London Transport*

Below: Brill, the end of the branch from Quainton Road. The old Metropolitan carriage No 232 is a 3rd class vehicle with, it appears, guard's van accommodation at the further end. Next to it is a milk van and behind is a Metropolitan four-wheeled brake van. In the siding on the left is a cattle wagon. Behind the station, in the distance, is Brill Hill through which the extension of the line to Oxford would have gone had this been carried out as had been originally intended. *Michael Crosby*

Above right: Winslow Road station in the early 1930s.
F. H. Stingemore courtesy London Transport

Below right: Verney Junction — the outermost extremity of the Metropolitan Railway where connection was made with the former LNWR Oxford to Bletchley line (sometimes known as the inter-varsity line). The station was named after Sir Harry Verney who was one of the promoters of what at one time was known as the Aylesbury and Buckingham Railway. He lived nearby at Claydon House and became a director of the Metropolitan. In this photograph, the Metropolitan line is on the left and that to Oxford is on the right. Metropolitan passenger services ceased in July 1936 whilst, on the inter-varsity line passenger trains continued to run until the beginning of 1938. The line from Quainton Road was singled in 1940 and was taken up completely shortly after the end of the last war. Today the only remaining connection with the Metropolitan line is the spur near Calvert which was installed during World War 2 and which is still used for freight traffic and also for routeing diesel multiple-units to and from Bletchley when in need of servicing. *F. H. Stingemore courtesy London Transport*

Above: In steam days Bletchley, like Reading, was one of those places where you never quite knew what to expect to see. Although, regrettably, I was only ever able to spend one day in and around Bletchley taking railway pictures, I was far from disappointed.

On my visit during the summer of 1938, locomotives of three pre-Grouping companies (LNW, LYR and Midland) were to be seen and were reasonably well positioned for photography. But it was the inter-varsity line which provided the most interesting subjects. It was at

Fenny Stratford, just outside Bletchley that I obtained my best picture of an ex-LNW 'Cauliflower' 0-6-0 No 8367 here seen on a train from Bedford. Of particular interest is the ex-Midland clerestory vehicle next behind the tender. No less interesting is the ex-Midland Johnson 0-4-4T No 1260, still with Salter safety valves, on a two-coach push-pull unit of ex-LNWR origin. This train was also operating between Bletchley and Bedford. *Both: C. R. L. Coles*

The 16.5 miles from Bletchley to Tring is almost continually on a rising gradient culminating in six miles at 1 in 333 to the summit just east of Tring station. From both intermediate stations — Leighton Buzzard and Cheddington — short branches deviated to Dunstable and Aylesbury (High Street) respectively.

Above: Ex-LNW Webb 2-4-2T No 46601 approaching Leighton Buzzard with a train from Dunstable on 11 May 1949. Passenger trains ceased to run from 30 June 1962 and the branch was closed completely at the end of 1965. *H. C. Casserley*

Below: Stanbridgeford was the only intermediate station on the Dunstable branch. This picture was taken from a train window on 26 May 1956 and, as can be seen, the line was double track. This extended from Leighton Buzzard to Dunstable North. *H. C. Casserley*

Above: Former LNW 0-8-0 No 49144 approaching Aylesbury (High Street) with a goods train from Cheddington whilst 2-4-2T No 46601 which had previously worked a passenger train up the branch stands on an adjacent track. This photograph was taken in 1950. The branch was closed in February 1953. *C. R. L. Coles*

Below: Ivatt 2-6-0 No 43002 (with double chimney) leaving Aylesbury (High Street) with a goods train for Cheddington and Bletchley on 8 March 1952. *Ian S. Pearsall*

Tring Cutting

Here the railway threads through the western escarpment of the Chiltern Downs where the chalk comes very close to the surface. This is shown very clearly on pp75, 76. This, like other similar cuttings in the Chilterns is also a nature reserve.

Below: Down Blackpool express headed by rebuilt 'Patriot' class 4-6-0 No 45735 *Comet* accelerating down the 1 in 333 through the cutting towards Cheddington. Photographed in April 1953. *C. R. L. Coles*

Above left: 'Jubilee' class 4-6-0 No 45721 *Impregnable* heading a down Northampton train through Tring Cutting in May 1952.   *C. R. L. Coles*

Below left: Stanier 2-8-0 No 48033 pauses beneath the signal gantry north of Tring station in September 1959. The upper quadrant signals, controlling up trains denoted, from right to left: (a) up fast; (b) up fast to up slow; (c) up fast to siding; (d) up slow; (e) up slow to siding. *C. R. L. Coles*

Above: The 'Coronation Scot' was introduced in 1937 to mark the Coronation of TM King George VI and Queen Elizabeth. It ran between London (Euston) and Glasgow and was the first fully streamlined train to appear on the LMSR. In this 1938 photograph, the up express is seen at Tring summit headed by 4-6-2 No 6224 *Princess Alexandra*. When World War 2 broke out in September 1939, this service was withdrawn.   *C. R. L. Coles*

Below: Breasting the summit at Tring. 'Royal Scot' class 4-6-0 No 6157 *The Royal Artilleryman* is here seen on an up Blackpool express in 1938.   *C. R. L. Coles*

Left: As evening draws on, an up Bletchley train leaves Tring hauled by an ex-LNWR 'Prince of Wales' class 4-6-0 the number of which is not known. Photographed in 1937. *C. R. L. Coles*

Below left: Up goods train at Tring summit hauled by a former LNW 0-8-0 No 9364. This photograph was taken in 1938. *C. R. L. Coles*

Right: An unidentified Fowler G3 0-8-0 approaching Tring summit in 1936 with a down mixed freight train. This class ended their days on the former Lancashire & Yorkshire Railway in and around Todmorden and Bacup. *C. R. L. Coles*

Below: The 'Sunny South Express' — through train on Saturdays during the summer season between the south coast and the Midlands — near Northchurch in 1938. An unidentified 'Black Five' 4-6-0 is heading a train composed of Southern Railway stock. *C. R. L. Coles*

The tragedy of Bourne End — 30 September 1945. It will never be known just why one of the overnight expresses from Scotland failed to reduce speed before reaching the point where, because of engineering work on the track, all up trains were being switched from the fast to slow line. The locomotive left the rails and overturned in a field of mangolds at the bottom of a 15ft embankment. Much of the train was also derailed. Before the locomotive could be recovered it was necessary to strengthen the embankment carrying the permanent way in order to take the weight of two steam cranes and that of the damaged engine. This work entailed the driving of steel piles into the ground which would support the outriggers of the two cranes. The task of recovering the engine was successfully accomplished on 28 October 1945. First, the engine had to be stood on its wheels on a temporary bed of sleepers before the main lift could begin. These four photographs show the different stages of this operation. The engine concerned was 4-6-0 No 6157 *The Royal Artilleryman* (see also p77). *C. R. L. Coles*

Above: A down local train from Euston to Tring photographed at Kings Langley on 7 September 1929. The locomotive is an ex-LNW 'Precursor' 4-4-2T No 6794. At that time a number of this class were allocated to Watford shed and of these, No 6794 was the only one which was painted in LMS crimson livery. The others were painted black. *E. R. Wethersett and from the collection of H. C. Casserley*

Below: Class 5 4-6-0 No 4826 passing Watford Junction in 1947 with a train of empty 40-ton coal wagons. These wagons worked to and from

the power station at Stonebridge Park and were fitted with the vacuum brake. *C. R. L. Coles*

Right: Sunday afternoon at Watford sheds. In this 1933 photograph, the ex-Midland 'Kirtley' 2-4-0 No 20008 had just completed a turn of duty either on a ballast train, or possibly, with an inspection saloon. The ex-LNW 0-8-0 No 9128, with steam up, had probably also completed a similar Sunday duty. This site is now a car park. *C. R. L. Coles*

HE STATION, BRICKET WOOD

Left: The Watford Junction to St Albans (Abbey) branch. These two photographs were both taken at Watford Junction, one in 1938; the other in May 1957. In the earlier picture, Stanier 0-4-4T No 6409 is attached to a two coach push-pull unit and is standing in platform 9. The later picture shows a lightweight three-car diesel unit standing at the same platform. *Both: C. R. L. Coles*

Above: Bricket Wood station on the St Albans branch. This early photograph, the date of which is not known shows a train from Watford Junction with a Webb 2-4-2T locomotive. In more recent years, this station was provided with a passing loop to enable two trains to operate over this branch.
Collection of H. C Casserley

Right: St Albans (Abbey) station was also the terminus of a former LNER branch from Hatfield. This picture, taken on 11 August 1945, shows a Gresley N2 class 0-6-2T No 4577 on a train for Hatfield. *H. C. Casserley*

Above left: The dc electric line from Watford Junction to Euston deviates via Watford High Street station before running parallel to the main line from Bushey to beyond Wembley. In this 1946 photograph a relaying gang is at work at the junction with the branches to Croxley Green (and the carriage sheds nearby) and Rickmansworth (Church Street). In attendance is Class 4 0-6-0 No 4372 which is standing on the branch to Croxley. Because of the sharp curve at this point, wear and tear over this junction is very considerable. *C. R. L. Coles*

Left: Beyond the carriage sheds the line divided into two single arms — one for Croxley Green; the other for Rickmansworth. This photograph, taken on 23 February 1952, just one week before this branch was closed to passenger traffic, shows a three-coach electric train of former LNW 'Oerlikon' stock approaching Rickmansworth station. One of the 'Oerlikon' motor cars, No 28249, is now preserved in the National Railway Museum at York in former LMS maroon livery. *C. R. L. Coles*

Top: When brought into service in the mid-1950s, the English Electric *Deltic* was rated as the most powerful locomotive yet to run on British Railways. Powered by Napier engines similar to those widely used by the Royal Navy, it was the forerunner of the fleet of 'Deltics' which have been in service for some years on the East Coast main line between Kings Cross and Edinburgh. The English Electric prototype was first used on the West Coast route between Euston and Liverpool. This 1957 photograph shows the locomotive passing Watford Junction with the down 'Shamrock'. It now rests in the Science Museum at South Kensington. *C. R. L. Coles*

Above: In this 1948 picture, rebuilt 'Patriot' class 4-6-0 No 45531 *Sir Frederick Harrison* is seen approaching Bushey station with an up express from Wolverhampton. The engine and carriage stock are painted in an experimental new style British Railways livery. *C. R. L. Coles*

Bushey Troughs

The water troughs south of Bushey station have always been a favourite spot for the railway photographer during the steam age. These five pictures cover a period of between 40 and 50 years from the time that LNWR 2-4-0s were still to be seen on express passenger trains until after Britain's railways became Nationalised in 1948.

Above left: LNWR 2-4-0s No 486 *Skiddaw* and No 2182 *Giraffe* double-heading an up express from Nuneaton. Circa 1910. *Locomotive Publishing Co Ltd*
Collection of C. R. L. Coles

Below left: Up Liverpool express hauled by an unidentified 'Claughton' class 4-6-0 in 1933.   *C. R. L. Coles*

Above: In this 1938 picture, the down 'Merseyside' express is headed by Stanier 4-6-2 No 6207 *Princess Arthur of Connaught*.   *C. R. L. Coles*

Below: The down 'Royal Scot' headed by Gresley A4 class No 60034 *Lord Faringdon* was photographed during the locomotive exchange trials in 1948 when this train (10am ex-Euston) was one of the selected trains to be hauled by 'foreign' locomotives.   *C. R. L. Coles*

Left: Rebuilt 'Royal Scot' class 4-6-0 No 46120 *Royal Inniskilling Fusilier* with a full tender of water is here seen approaching Bushey station in May 1952 with the down 'Comet'. *C. R. L. Coles*

Above: The Royal Train en route from Euston to Ballater in August 1939, passing Carpenders Park headed by 'Coronation' class 4-6-2 No 6225 *Duchess of Gloucester*. At that time this train was still resplendent in the former LNWR livery — plum and spilt milk. During World War II it was, for security reasons, painted in the same style as that of ordinary LMS stock. *C. R. L. Coles*

Below: USA Austerity 2-8-0 No 2415 is here seen on a down goods train near Hatch End in 1944. *C. R. L. Coles*

Left: An evening picture of 'Jubilee' class 4-6-0 No 45688 *Polyphemus* heading the down 'Midlander' near Hatch End in June 1953. *C. R. L. Coles*

Above: An up semi-fast train from Northampton hauled by former

LNWR 'Prince of Wales' class 4-6-0 No 25673 *Lusitania* approaching Headstone Lane in 1938. *C. R. L. Coles*

Below: Stanier 2-6-4T No 2589 photographed at Headstone Lane in 1938 on an evening commuter train — Euston to Tring. *C. R. L. Coles*

Above: By Underground to the Chilterns! An early morning scene at Harrow & Wealdstone station in 1946. The train at platform 1 is composed of pre-1938 Bakerloo Line stock some of which was, at that time, allocated to the Croxley Green carriage depot. In this picture it is en route for Watford Junction. *C. R. L. Coles*

Left: Her Majesty's Mail. In this photograph, taking in June 1947, the 'West Coast Postal' which, at that time left Euston nightly at 8.30pm, is about to collect mail from the lineside apparatus south of Harrow & Wealdstone station. Similar pick-up points were located further down the line — at Watford, Boxmoor and Tring. Because of the time of evening, this was the best place for photography due to the absence of cuttings or other nearby buildings which would considerably reduce the amount of available daylight. This practice ceased to operate as from the beginning of 1971. *C. R. L. Coles*

Above right: Fresh from the shops. 'Patriot' class 4-6-0 No 45517 heading a vacuum fitted express goods train is here seen crossing over to the down fast line at Wembley Central on the first stage of its journey north through the Chilterns to Crewe and beyond. Photograph taken in May 1958. *C. R. L. Coles*

Right: A view looking towards London from Wembley Central and photographed in May 1964. The steel supports for the overhead electric catenary cables are already in position. A diesel-electric locomotive hauling a train of Ford covered container vans is approaching on the down relief line whilst 2-6-4T No 42118 is in the siding to the left. On the extreme right of the picture is the dc electric line from Euston on which a Bakerloo train is seen approaching from Stonebridge Park. *C. R. L. Coles*

Above left: 'Royal Scot' class 4-6-0 No 6114
Coldstream Guardsman tops Camden incline
with an express for Birmingham and
Wolverhampton. This first mile out of Euston is
at an inclination of 1 in 70/77 for part of the
distance after which there are no gradients
steeper than 1 in 330 before reaching Tring
summit. But unlike the approaches to the
Chilterns via the Midland or Great Central
routes both of which are more undulating, there
was little respite for an engine on a fast express.
This could, at times, be somewhat trying
especially with an engine starting a long non-
stop run in a 'cold' condition. Photographed in
1938. *C. R. L. Coles*

Below left: The down 'Midday Scot' on Camden
Bank headed by 4-6-2 No 6201 *Princess
Elizabeth* with banking assistance in the rear.
Photograph taken in 1938. *C. R. L. Coles*

Above: The up 'Caledonian' at Euston, platform
3 on 17 May 1957 at the conclusion of the
inaugural run from Glasgow. With the driver
and fireman is Station Master Turrell. The
locomotive is 4-6-2 No 46229 *Duchess of
Hamilton*. *Hugh B. Oliver*

Right: Another picture of Euston before the
station was completely rebuilt during the 1960s.
This pre-1939 photograph was taken on
Platform 2 whilst the down 'West Coast Postal'
was being loaded with mail. The train would be
brought into the station shortly after 7 o'clock
in the evening after which the platform was a
hive of activity until just before departure at
8.30pm. *C. R. L. Coles*

St Pancras to Hemel Hempstead, Luton and Bedford; Dunstable to Hertford; St Margarets to Hertford East; the Hertford loop to Langley Junction then returning via Welwyn to Kings Cross

'The Midland was a magnificent railway'. So wrote that well-known railway historian — Cuthbert Hamilton Ellis in his excellent book *The Midland Railway*. Which just about sums it up admirably. It was, in terms of mileage, the third largest in the country and was (indeed still is) one of the three main transport arteries linking London with the industrial north. Certain features peculiar to the Midland survived for many years after the Grouping. Others survive today.

One very noticeable feature was that, unlike the LNWR or, to a lesser extent, the Great Northern, Midland locomotives were smaller. Yet it managed to provide a service, both passenger and freight, of which it could be justly proud. Double-heading was therefore widely adopted and this practice continued, more especially with heavy coal trains, until several years after the Grouping when the Beyer-Garratts and Stanier 2-8-0s took over these duties from the pairs of 0-6-0 maids-of-all-work which had up until then, performed yeoman service.

For express passenger trains, the 4-4-0 reigned supreme (sometimes in tandem) and of which the best remembered are the Deeley compounds. Although my picture of No 1000, the class leader, as now preserved, was taken at Marylebone in 1961, I felt that I *had* to fit it into this group somehow. What a glorious sight she must have been at the head of a set of David Bain's clerestory carriages, all gleaming in Midland lake, topping the 1 in 176 at Elstree — the first of two summits on the approach to the Chilterns from London and a favourite spot for the railway photographer. But it was the heavy coal trains that provided the best sight of all as they toiled up the 1 in 200 from Radlett. With sometimes as much as 1,200 tons behind the tender, the locomotives were certainly panting when they reached the summit.

But as a curtain raiser to this, the final group of pictures, I am, by way of a diversion, including one of a series taken at St Pancras one Sunday in 1947 when, in order to renew the approaches to the terminus, it was necessary to suspend all traffic whilst this work was being undertaken. Each section of new track which had previously been pre-assembled could then be correctly positioned in sequence after removal of the old track. So, back to No 1000, the ex-LNW 'Claughtons', 'Patriots', 'Jubilees', 'Black Fives' and finally the rebuilt 'Scots' all of

which recall progress on the Midland as we turn the pages of this album on our tour of Chiltern country.

Few photographs appear to have been taken at Napsbury which lay well off the beaten track. Perhaps this was just as well as the station served a nearby mental hospital to which a short branch diverged from the main line. However, by the kindness of Mr Hugh B. Oliver of Mill Hill, I am able to include a photograph taken at Napsbury station on the day of closure. Both station and branch no longer exist today.

So to St Albans, best known for its abbey which also has cathedral status. In style and appearance, more especially when seen from inside, it is very similar to that of Winchester — particularly the very long nave, characteristic of the Norman period, and the 15th century reredos. There is also time for a refresher at the nearby 'Fighting Cocks', reputed to be the oldest licensed house in England, before proceeding to Harpenden for a trip down the branch to Hemel Hempstead and Heath Park Halt. The branch, with run round facilities, continued beyond this halt into a gasworks almost adjacent to Boxmoor station on the main line from Euston. There was no physical connection between the two except for a very short while prior to the changeover from coal gas to natural gas. Only a part of the branch at the Harpenden end remains intact and its use is confined to industrial purposes. Luton, home of Vauxhalls and of the boater (seldom seen nowadays except during term time at Harrow School) is near the summit of this route through the Chilterns after which the gradient falls at 1 in 200 for most of the way to Bedford.

Like the former LNW branch to Dunstable North where end-on connection was made with the LNE line from Hatfield and Welwyn Garden City, this latter can be regarded as typical of many country branch lines where, in the more rural districts, everybody knew one another almost as though they were brothers. It was a part of village life — part of the community. Here, on some evenings, after the last train for the day had gone, Harry, stationmaster-cum-signalman-cum-booking clerk; Bob, his assistant and general factotum and George, the landlord of the nearby inn would all be enjoying a pint of the best brew. The vicar too, he wasn't going to be left out either — pastoral duties permitting! But those days are now but a memory of the distant past. Like many others, this branch — apart from the section between Luton and Dunstable over which infrequent freight traffic is worked by the London Midland Region — no longer exists. On the latest ordnance survey map, a thin dotted line marked 'course of old rly' is all there is to remind us that a railway *did* serve this part of rural Hertfordshire. Another branch from Welwyn Garden City went in an easterly direction via Cole Green to Hertford North and it also made connection with the line from Liverpool Street to Hertford East just beyond that station. This branch, too, is now extinct.

The Hertford loop line to and from Kings Cross provides an alternative route to the direct line via Welwyn whenever engineering operations necessitate diversion of long distance trains. From Langley Junction where this line rejoins the former, the gradient continues at 1 in 200 over the eastern shoulder of the downs near Knebworth before falling at a similar inclination to Hitchin. A few miles to the east, at the foot of one of the more isolated areas of downland lies Buntingford which, until September 1965, was served by the former Great Eastern Railway branch from St Margarets. This branch followed a somewhat meandering route amongst the leafy lanes of rural Hertfordshire to this small Chiltern outpost. I am happy that of the two pictures in this album taken in the Lea Valley near St Margarets, one of them should feature this branch. But now it is back to Welwyn Garden City for the concluding run direct to Kings Cross.

But this is not quite the end of the series. The eclipse of steam has witnessed many 'last days' in countless places. The final page in this album which, appropriately, has been titled 'Steam Finale', shows two such photographs recalling such occasions.

Above: Renewal of approach lines to St Pancras station. In this photograph taken in June 1947, a steam crane is seen lowering a prefabricated section of new track into its correct position.
C. R. L. Coles

Left: Deeley 3-cylinder compound 4-4-0 No 1000 restored to its original condition and former Midland livery on view at Marylebone goods station in 1961. *C. R. L. Coles*

Top: Former LNWR 'Claughton' class 4-6-0 No 6025 at St Pancras station. This and the picture below recall the introduction of larger

express passenger locomotives to the Midland division of the LMSR following the Grouping in 1923. *Collection of H. C. Casserley*

Above: Former 'Claughton' class 4-6-0 No 6001 passing Hendon with the 3.30pm express from St Pancas to Leeds. The exact date of this picture is not known. *Collection of H. C. Casserley*

Above: Next to appear on the Midland division were one or two 'Patriot' class 4-6-0s. In this 1938 photograph, No 5538 is approaching Elstree on a down Manchester express. *C. R. L. Coles*

Below: In the late 1930s both Stanier 2-cylinder and 3-cylinder 4-6-0s made their appearance on expresses to and from St Pancras. In this 1953 photograph, 'Jubilee' class 4-6-0 No 45611 *Hong Kong* is approaching the south end of Elstree Tunnel with a down Bradford

express. At this point the down line is on a rising gradient of 1 in 176 to the summit near Elstree station — the first of two summits on this route through the Chilterns. *C. R. L. Coles*

Right: In this photograph taken in May 1952, 4-6-0 No 45608 *Gibraltar* is emerging from Elstree Tunnel with a down Bradford express. The summit is about half a mile from this point. *C. R. L. Coles*

Above left: Representing the Stanier 'Black Fives' I have chosen one of a batch which were fitted with Caprotti gear instead of the usual Walschaerts gear. This modification did not improve the general appearance of these engines. No 44755 is here seen approaching Elstree on a down train of milk empties in June 1955. *C. R. L. Coles*

Left: My only picture of a rebuilt 'Royal Scot' in this area was taken at Mill Hill in July 1960. No 46112 *Sherwood Forester* is here seen heading the down 'Robin Hood' on a sunny evening. *C. R. L. Coles*

Above: On the same evening and at the same place I obtained this picture of the diesel operated 'Midland Pullman' en route from St Pancras to Manchester Central. Like the 'Birmingham Pullman' this was one of the prestige business trains linking London with the Midlands and Lancashire during the period that the former LNWR main line was being electrified. *C. R. L. Coles*

Right: Mill Hill station with the up 'Palatine' approaching in August 1958. This photograph shows the typical style of Midland architecture featured at some stations. Similar styles were also to be found at Elstree and Bedford. Here, at Mill Hill the station has, in recent years, been rebuilt and this truly Midland greenhouse style no longer exists. *Hugh B. Oliver*

Above left: No 1015 — one of the original batch of Deeley compounds — had seen more than 40 years' service when this photograph was taken in 1948. The engine was working an up excursion train and is here seen approaching Elstree Tunnel. *C. R. L. Coles*

Left: Further locomotives of similar design to the Deeley compounds were built by the LMSR. However, they differed from the earlier series in that they were fitted for left hand drive whilst the coupled wheels had a diameter of 6ft 9in instead of 7ft 0in. No 1091 of the later series hauling an unidentified express was photographed at Elstree during the winter freeze up of 1947. *C. R. L. Coles*

Top: Another of the later compounds, No 41049, with a down Bedford train is here seen emerging from Elstree Tunnel in June 1955. *C. R. L. Coles*

Above: Built in 1900 but subsequently rebuilt with superheater, Johnson 4-4-0 No 707 was photographed on an up parcels train near Elstree Tunnel in 1938. *C. R. L. Coles*

Above left: A pre-1923 photograph of an up coal train approaching the summit at Elstree and hauled by Johnson Class 3 0-6-0 No 3344 piloted by Johnson Class 2 0-6-0 No 2963. *H. C. Casserley*

Left: This photograph which was taken in 1936 from the footbridge seen in the picture above shows Johnson rebuilt Class 3 0-6-0 No 3797 piloting another of the same class on an up coal train. A cold northerly wind and bright early spring sunshine have produced the remarkable effect of rapidly condensing exhaust at the moment that the train engine was immediately under the overbridge. Entitled *Smoke and Steam*, this picture was awarded a certificate of merit in the 22nd Kodak International Salon of Photography which was held in Paris in 1957. *C. R. L. Coles*

Above: Stanier 2-8-0 No 8191 with a train of empty coal wagons bound for the Nottinghamshire coalfields photographed when approaching Elstree in 1948. Like the 'Jubilee' class 4-6-0s, they incorporated 'Swindon' features in their design. *C. R. L. Coles*

Right: Old Midland Railway notice in cast iron. This plate is dated 1875 and was photographed near Radlett. *C. R. L. Coles*

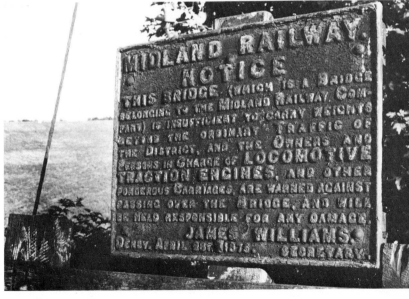

Left: Beyer-Garratt 2-6-0+0-6-2 No 7988 approaching Elstree station with an up coal train from Toton to Brent. Photographed in March 1939. *C. R. L. Coles*

Below left: Up coal train entering Elstree Tunnel in 1955 headed by BR 2-10-0 No 92045. *C. R. L. Coles*

Right: BR Standard Class 5 4-6-0 No 73018 on a down Nottingham express approaching Radlett in June 1952. From here the line is on a rising gradient of 1 in 176 to St Albans. *C. R. L. Coles*

Below right: Napsbury station closed for passenger trains on 14 September 1959. In this photograph, the last down train to stop here is seen approaching the station. *Hugh B. Oliver*

Above left: Harpenden Junction — 18 April 1959. The branch to Hemel Hempstead deviates to the left, the main line continues straight ahead. Note the 12mph speed restriction sign south of the cross-over beyond the bridge. Note also the signalbox partly hidden behind one of the bridge supports. This junction is still intact as a short section of the branch gives access to an industrial plant. *Hugh B. Oliver*

Left: Harpenden-Hemel Hempstead branch. This photograph taken on 18 April 1959 shows Beaumonts Halt looking towards Harpenden. Note the overgrown state of both track and platform. *Hugh B. Oliver*

Above: In August 1958 the Railway Correspondence & Travel Society organised a rail tour which included the branch line to Hemel Hempstead. Except for a short length at the Harpenden Junction end, the branch was closed completely in the following year and the track taken up. Major changes in the environment have since taken place — more especially in the Hemel Hempstead area. The administrative offices of Kodak Limited, an 18-storey structure and a prominent landmark, now occupy the site of what, at that time, was Heath Park Halt where this photograph was taken. The locomotive is an ex-Midland Class 3 0-6-0 No 43245. Note also the much overgrown state of the track. *C. R. L. Coles*

Right: Heath Park Halt on the Hemel Hempstead branch. Photographed on 18 April 1959 looking towards Harpenden just before closure. The daily goods train can be seen shunting in the distance. *Hugh B. Oliver*

Top: Chiltern Green for Luton Hoo station in July 1939. A 'Jubilee' class 4-6-0 No 5614 *Leeward Islands* is here seen heading a down express freight train.   *H. C. Casserley*

Above: Luton station with a down Manchester express approaching hauled by 'Jubilee' class 4-6-0 No 45615 *Malay States* on 14 June 1959.   *Hugh B. Oliver*

Above right: Harlington (Beds). No 757, one of the Johnson Class 3 superheated 4-4-0s is heading a down express on 7 June 1939. In the siding on the left of the picture is a Johnson Class 4 superheated 0-6-0 believed to be No 3857.   *H. C. Casserley*

Right: Johnson 2-4-0 No 20251 standing in Bedford (Midland Road) station in June 1939. Note also the 'Inverted Greenhouse' style of Midland station architecture similar to that which once was at Mill Hill.   *C. R. L. Coles*

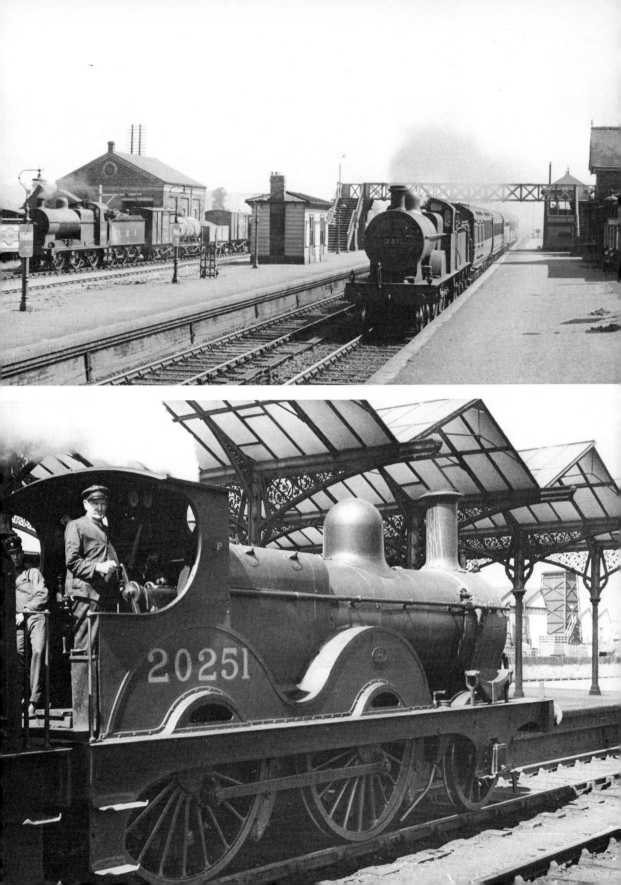

The former LNER branch line from Hatfield and Welwyn Garden City to Dunstable

Top: Dunstable North station on 24 September 1955. Gresley N2 0-6-2T locomotive No 69504 heading a goods train awaiting the arrival of No 69654 of the same class with a passenger train from Welwyn and Hatfield. *H. C. Casserley*

Above: N2 0-6-2T No 2648 on a passenger train between Luton (Bute Street) and Harpenden East on 13 July 1939. This section of the branch, between Luton and Hatfield, was closed on 24 April 1965. *H. C. Casserley*

Above right: Wheathampstead station looking west — June 1960. *J. Spencer Gilks*

Right: Ayot loop looking east — June 1960. At one time a station existed here. *J. Spencer Gilks*

Top: View looking north in June 1960 showing the approach to Welwyn from the Luton direction on the left with the main line from Kings Cross on the right. When this branch was first opened, it made connection with the main line at Welwyn Junction (near the site of the present Welwyn Garden City station). This junction was later closed and the branch extended on a parallel independent single line to Hatfield which then became the starting point for trains to Luton and beyond except those working to and from London. *J. Spencer Gilks*

Above: Looking south towards Welwyn Garden City station with Brush diesel-electric locomotive No D5300 drawing out of the down platform with empty stock. The outer face of the platform on the left was used by trains to and from Hertford North. The corresponding side of the down platform was used by trains to and from Luton and/or Dunstable — the track passing behind the signalbox. *C. R. L. Coles*

Scenes on the branch between Hertford North and Welwyn Garden City

Top: REC special headed by 0-6-2T No 69514 photographed near Hertingfordbury on 15 June 1957. Passenger services on this branch were withdrawn as an economy measure in June 1951. This branch is now extinct and recent road works have entirely obliterated the track bed near here. *J. Spencer Gilks*

Above: The down platform at Cole Green photographed from the REC special on the same day. *J. Spencer Gilks*

Above: The former Great Eastern Railway gained access to the Chilterns at Hertford via the Lea Valley — a branch diverging from the Cambridge line at Broxbourne Junction with intermediate stations at St Margarets and Ware. St Margarets was also the junction for the Buntingford branch which, for a short distance, ran parallel to the Hertford line. These two photographs, taken near St Margarets on the same day in 1947, depict N7 class 0-6-2T No 9682 on a Liverpool Street to Hertford East train and a former Holden 2-4-2T No 7220 on the Buntingford branch train. The latter was closed on 20 September 1965. *Both C. R. L. Coles*

Right: Ex-GNR steam rail motor No 5 at Hertford North in July 1924. This and No 6 of the same type were used for a short while on the Hertford-Stevenage and Hitchin service. It would appear that they did not give satisfactory service and were replaced by steam locomotives hauling two-coach units (see overleaf).
A. W. Croughton/Eric Neve collection

Top: Ex-GNR D2 class 4-4-0 No 4326 on train from Hitchin to Hertford North being overtaken by an express for Kings Cross headed by CI class 4-4-2 No 4407; c1926/27. *Rail Archive Stephenson*

Above: Six-cylinder 'Sentinel' steam railcar No 51914 *Royal Forester* near Langley Junction on the same service. This and a Clayton steam railcar were introduced to this duty in 1928/29 and continued to work the service until September 1939 when it ceased to operate. *Collection of Eric Neve*

Above right: The 2.21pm Kings Cross to Cambridge train headed by B17 class 4-6-0 No 61652 *Darlington* approaching Stapleford station on 13 September 1953. Because of engineering work, necessitating complete occupation of the track on the direct line via Welwyn, all trains were being diverted via Hertford North. *J. F. Aylard*

Right: Up express from Hull hauled by A3 class 4-6-2 No 60067 *Ladas* approaching Stapleford station on the same day. *J. F. Aylard*

Above left: The 3.30pm stopping train from Kings Cross, hauled by C1 class 4-4-2 No 4441, breasting the 1 in 200 over the eastern shoulder of the downs north of Knebworth. Here, the chalk layer is very close to the surface and can clearly be seen to the left of the locomotive; c1926/27. *Rail Archive Stephenson*

Left: The 300ft contour crosses the main line from Kings Cross about one mile north of Welwyn Garden City station and again at Welwyn North station. The valley between these two points is approximately half a mile wide and, at its deepest part, is spanned by Digswell Viaduct — nearly 100ft in height above the valley floor. Through this valley flows the River Maran or Mimram in a south-easterly direction to Hertford where it links up with the Rivers Lea and Beane. *C. R. L. Coles*

Top: In September 1938, Patrick Stirling's 4-2-2 locomotive No 1 was brought out of the old York Museum and prepared for steaming in readiness to work a six-coach replica of the 1888 'Flying Scotsman' express which, in that year, was celebrating its Golden Jubilee. The replica train was also chartered by the Railway Correspondence and Travel Society for a trip to Peterborough and back. In this photograph, No 1 is seen passing Potters Bar on the northbound journey. *C. R. L. Coles*

Above: Up local train at Ganwick in 1938 hauled by former GN D3 class 4-4-0 No 3049. *C. R. L. Coles*

Above: 'Garden Cities Express' — Cambridge to Kings Cross — passing Hadley Wood in 1938 headed by rebuilt B12 class 4-6-0 No 8530 in LNER apple green livery. These trains were locally referred to as 'beer trains'. *C. R. L. Coles*

Below: The down 'Yorkshire Pullman' approaching Greenwood Tunnel in 1949 headed by Thompson A2 class 4-6-2 No 60513 *Dante*. *C. R. L. Coles*

Right: Kings Cross — scene of many historical departures in yesteryear. In this photograph which was taken on 20 September 1953, the two preserved GNR Atlantic locomotives No 251 and No 990 *Henry Oakley* heading the 'Plant Centenarian' are about to enter Gas Works Tunnel on that memorable journey to Doncaster. *C. R. L. Coles*

Steam Finale

Above: On 11 September 1960, the London Transport Chesham branch shuttle train was steam operated for the last time — the locomotive on duty being British Railways 2-6-2T No 41284. It is here seen propelling a rake of three ex-Metropolitan 'Ashbury' coaches towards Chesham. As on many other 'last day' occasions, the train was well filled for every journey. *C. R. L. Coles*

Below: The 4.15pm semi-fast train from Paddington to Banbury photographed on 11 June 1965 between Beaconsfield and High Wycombe (with White House Farm Tunnel in the background) headed by 'Castle' class 4-6-0 No 7029 *Clun Castle*. This was the last regular steam hauled train then operating in the London area. *Gerald T. Robinson*